U.S. POLICY IN THE PACIFIC: THE STRUGGLE TO MAINTAIN INFLUENCE

HEARING

BEFORE THE

SUBCOMMITTEE ON ASIA AND THE PACIFIC

OF THE

COMMITTEE ON FOREIGN AFFAIRS
HOUSE OF REPRESENTATIVES

ONE HUNDRED FOURTEENTH CONGRESS

SECOND SESSION

JUNE 23, 2016

Serial No. 114–176

Printed for the use of the Committee on Foreign Affairs

Available via the World Wide Web: http://www.foreignaffairs.house.gov/ or
http://www.gpo.gov/fdsys/

U.S. GOVERNMENT PUBLISHING OFFICE

20–532PDF   WASHINGTON : 2016

COMMITTEE ON FOREIGN AFFAIRS

EDWARD R. ROYCE, California, *Chairman*

CHRISTOPHER H. SMITH, New Jersey
ILEANA ROS-LEHTINEN, Florida
DANA ROHRABACHER, California
STEVE CHABOT, Ohio
JOE WILSON, South Carolina
MICHAEL T. McCAUL, Texas
TED POE, Texas
MATT SALMON, Arizona
DARRELL E. ISSA, California
TOM MARINO, Pennsylvania
JEFF DUNCAN, South Carolina
MO BROOKS, Alabama
PAUL COOK, California
RANDY K. WEBER SR., Texas
SCOTT PERRY, Pennsylvania
RON DeSANTIS, Florida
MARK MEADOWS, North Carolina
TED S. YOHO, Florida
CURT CLAWSON, Florida
SCOTT DesJARLAIS, Tennessee
REID J. RIBBLE, Wisconsin
DAVID A. TROTT, Michigan
LEE M. ZELDIN, New York
DANIEL DONOVAN, New York

ELIOT L. ENGEL, New York
BRAD SHERMAN, California
GREGORY W. MEEKS, New York
ALBIO SIRES, New Jersey
GERALD E. CONNOLLY, Virginia
THEODORE E. DEUTCH, Florida
BRIAN HIGGINS, New York
KAREN BASS, California
WILLIAM KEATING, Massachusetts
DAVID CICILLINE, Rhode Island
ALAN GRAYSON, Florida
AMI BERA, California
ALAN S. LOWENTHAL, California
GRACE MENG, New York
LOIS FRANKEL, Florida
TULSI GABBARD, Hawaii
JOAQUIN CASTRO, Texas
ROBIN L. KELLY, Illinois
BRENDAN F. BOYLE, Pennsylvania

AMY PORTER, *Chief of Staff*   THOMAS SHEEHY, *Staff Director*
JASON STEINBAUM, *Democratic Staff Director*

———

SUBCOMMITTEE ON ASIA AND THE PACIFIC

MATT SALMON, Arizona *Chairman*

DANA ROHRABACHER, California
STEVE CHABOT, Ohio
TOM MARINO, Pennsylvania
JEFF DUNCAN, South Carolina
MO BROOKS, Alabama
SCOTT PERRY, Pennsylvania
SCOTT DesJARLAIS, Tennessee

BRAD SHERMAN, California
AMI BERA, California
TULSI GABBARD, Hawaii
ALAN S. LOWENTHAL, California
GERALD E. CONNOLLY, Virginia
GRACE MENG, New York

CONTENTS

U.S. POLICY IN THE PACIFIC:
THE STRUGGLE TO MAINTAIN INFLUENCE

THURSDAY, JUNE 23, 2016

House of Representatives,
Subcommittee on Asia and the Pacific,
Committee on Foreign Affairs,
Washington, DC.

The subcommittee met, pursuant to notice, at 2:12 p.m., in room 2172, Rayburn House Office Building, Hon. Matt Salmon (chairman of the subcommittee) presiding.

Mr. SALMON. The subcommittee will come to order.

Members present will be permitted to submit written statements to be included in the official hearing record.

Without objection, the hearing record will remain open for 5 calendar days to allow statements, questions, and extraneous materials for the record subject to the length limitation in the rules.

The Pacific Island region, far from both the mainland United States and the core of Asia, is perhaps the most overlooked region of the Asia-Pacific. This cluster of 14 sovereign states, although home to only 9 million people, nevertheless deserves the United States' attention for the important roles that they play in regional security, as participants in international organizations, and as the neighbors to our own U.S. territories of American Samoa, Guam, and the Commonwealth of the Northern Mariana Islands in the Pacific.

I welcome the Delegates to Congress from the U.S. Pacific territories who have joined the hearing today. Thank you for coming. We appreciate your attendance.

Many of us remember the Pacific Island countries for the role they played during World War II. Following the war, the United States administered a number of the Pacific Islands under an arrangement with the United Nations. This included three now independent nations, Palau, the Marshall Islands, and Federated States of Micronesia, with signed a Compact of Free Association with the United States of America.

The United States maintains a specific relationship with these three countries today, including important military ties. The Marshall Islands, for example, hosts the vital Ronald Reagan Ballistic Missile Defense Test Site, which provides regional radar centers and launch sites. Our strategic planners following World War II also recognized the importance of the Pacific Islands to regional security, developing the island chain defense theory where our U.S.

territories and compact states form the second island chain defensive line.

The Pacific Island states are also of economic interest, especially for the U.S. fishing industry and as the South Pacific supplies roughly one-third of the world's tuna. For the past 28 years, the U.S. tuna fleet has gained access to these rich fishing grounds under the South Pacific Tuna Treaty, which exchanged fishing rights for licensing fees and $20 million in U.S. aid. Earlier this year, the United States suspended the treaty as the terms were ''no longer viable.'' The treaty is now under renegotiation, and I look forward to hearing from our witnesses about our efforts to support U.S. business and jobs in this important treaty negotiation.

We are not alone in recognizing the importance of the Pacific Island nations. Our friends in Australia and New Zealand play an active role as major donors and in promoting peace and security in the Pacific Islands region as they work to maintain a good relationship with their neighbors.

France, which also maintains territories in the South Pacific, plays an active role in the region as well. But not all new activity in the Pacific Island region is aligned with our interests. Five years ago, the Secretary of State Hillary Clinton testified to Congress that the United States was in direct competition for influence in the Pacific Island region. But very little seems to have been done since then to bolster our position. Beijing, on the other hand, has made significant advances. It has opened new Embassies in the Pacific Islands, provided an average of $150 million per year in economic assistance and established a strategic partnership with eight Pacific Island countries. China has started providing military training and equipment to some Pacific Island countries, and the People's Liberation Army frequently refers to the island chains in their own planning documents.

Chinese trade with the Pacific Island states is nearly 10 times larger than the United States. China has targeted the Pacific Islands in its diplomatic efforts. Vanuatu, a country that qualified for U.S. Millennium Challenge Corporation compact in 2006, is one of only eight countries to publicly back China's position that arbitration in the South China Sea is illegitimate. Although China is working to gain ground in the Pacific, the United States and its friends still maintain solid relationships there.

I do want to recognize the Pacific Island nations of Kiribati, the Marshall Islands, Nauru, Palau, the Solomon Islands, and Tuvalu for maintaining full diplomatic relations with Taiwan. That, to me, is very, very important and near and dear to my heart. In light of this competition between the United States and China in the Pacific, how is the United States faring as it struggles to maintain its longstanding influence in this important region? Have we devoted adequate resources to the Pacific Islands as part of the administration's rebalance?

I look forward to hearing from our witnesses on these issues, and I am going to refer, first of all, to the other member on the committee before I go to our guest today, so, Mr. Perry, did you have an opening statement you would like to make?

Mr. PERRY. Thanks, Mr. Chairman. I really don't. I didn't want to waste the time of everybody so I want to hear from the witnesses, but I appreciate the opportunity.

Mr. SALMON. Okay, well, great. We have a couple of guests today, and I will first turn to Congressman Sablan. It is customary to recognize the other sides of the aisle in the next statement, so we welcome any opening statements you would like to make.

Mr. SABLAN. Well, thank you very much, Chairman Salmon. I got promoted to ranking member just like this in probably my second invitation to this committee.

But, Chairman, thank you very much for inviting me to participate in today's hearing on the struggle to maintain United States influence in the Pacific. Before I continue on, I would like to recognize in the room the presence of the Dean of the Diplomatic Corps, the Ambassador of the Republic of Palau to the United States, Ambassador Kyota.

Ambassador, welcome.

Mr. Chairman, you could say that I am a Member of Congress today because of America's decision over half a century ago to maintain its influence in the Pacific. After World War II, the United Nations created a Trust Territory of the Pacific Islands out of islands that the United States had fought the Japanese for and the United States took responsibility for incorporating those islands into our Nation or giving them a path to independence.

The people of the Northern Mariana Islands voted to join the United States in 1976 and became U.S. citizens 10 years later. And as of 2009, the people of the Northern Marianas are represented alongside other Americans here in this House of Representatives, the seat I now hold. So America's influence in the Marianas, part of the Pacific, an area the size of California and Oregon combined, by the way, is secure. The people of the other three districts of the trust territory, however, chose independence. These new independent nations were created in free association with the United States. If we want to maintain influence in the Pacific, I believe then it is particularly important to focus on keeping those existing relationships with America strong. And I am very concerned about the relationship with one of those nations, the Republic of Palau.

The relationship is based on a Compact of Free Association, which established Palau's existence as an independent nation. The compact also pledged United States' economic support for the new republic and gave the United States exclusive military rights in the land and waters of Palau. The original compact, negotiated in 1994, also calls for a renewal of the agreement after 15 years. And, in 2010, the U.S. Representatives signed the renewal updating and extending the provisions of the compact for another 15 years.

Unfortunately, however, 6 years later, that agreement to extend the compact has not been approved by Congress. So, instead of giving Palau the assurance of a long-term commitment, we have been sending assistance to Palau on an installment basis, year by year. From the point of view of the Republic of Palau, you can imagine how this appears. It seems as though the United States is not good for its word. From my point of view, the people of Palau are very patient people. But patience has its limits. From the point of view of Palau's neighboring nations, imagine how America's unfulfilled promise appears? This is no way for our Nation to maintain influence on what is becoming, every day, a more strategically important and contested area of the world.

To address our unfulfilled promise, I introduced legislation in this Congress to approve the 15-year extension of America's compact with Palau. My legislation would make up to Palau for the financial assistance that it would have received under the extension agreement but which it has lost because of the Congress' inability to act. And to further push for resolution, in December, a group of Members from the Pacific—Ms. Bordallo of Guam, Ms. Gabbard and Mr. Takai of Hawaii and I—asked the Defense Department to support including the compact extension in the 2017 National Defense Authorization Act. And I understand the Defense Department has now reached out to both the House and Senate Armed Services Committees supporting resolution of the Palau issue in this year's NDAA. Hawaii Senator Mazie Hirono was also able to include in the Senate-passed defense bill this month a sense of Congress statement calling for resolution of the Palau issue.

The Defense Department sent letters, and Senator Hirono's amendments are important signals that we may be ready to get the congressional approval of the Palau Compact extension, but we have to get to the finish line in this Congress. And I am glad to report the chairman Bishop of the Natural Resources has agreed to hold a hearing on my bill approving the compact extension on July 6. And the hearing today, shining a light on America's struggle to maintain influence in the Pacific, can also help us reach our goal.

Mr. Chairman, I congratulate you for your decision to hold this hearing, and again, I thank you very much for inviting me to be here.

And I yield back my time.

Mr. SALMON. Thank you. We are very grateful to be joined today by Mr. Matt Matthews, the Deputy Assistant Secretary for Australia, New Zealand, and the Pacific Islands, as well as senior official for APEC in the State Department's Bureau of East Asian and Pacific Affairs—welcome—and Ms. Gloria Steele, the Senior Deputy Assistant Administrator in the U.S. Agency for International Development's Bureau for Asia.

And we thank the panel for joining us today to share their experience.

We will start with you, Mr. Matthews.

STATEMENT OF MR. MATTHEW J. MATTHEWS, DEPUTY ASSISTANT SECRETARY FOR AUSTRALIA, NEW ZEALAND, AND THE PACIFIC ISLANDS, SENIOR OFFICIAL FOR APEC, BUREAU OF EAST ASIAN AND PACIFIC AFFAIRS, U.S. DEPARTMENT OF STATE

Mr. MATTHEWS. Thank you, Mr. Chairman.

Mr. Chairman, Ranking Member Sherman, and members of the subcommittee, thank you for the opportunity to testify on U.S. public policy toward the Pacific Island countries and for your leadership on these issues. The Pacific Island region has been free of great power conflict since the end of World War II, and we have enjoyed friendly relations with all of the Pacific Island countries.

This state of affairs, however, is not guaranteed. Our partnerships and engagement in the region matter very greatly. Today, we partner together on a number of issues of global importance from standing together for human rights in the U.N. and contributing to global security through peacekeeping operations to combating climate change and illegal, unreported, and unregulated fishing.

The Pacific Islanders punch above their weight, and the United States must continue to encourage them through our support for their sustainable and inclusive development. However, it is equally important that we do not take Pacific goodwill for granted. Our relationship with our Pacific partners are unfolding against the backdrop of a shifting strategic environment where emerging powers in Asia and elsewhere seek to exert a greater influence in the Pacific region through development and economic aid, people-to-people contacts and security cooperation. There is continued uncertainty in the region about the United States' willingness and ability to sustain a robust forward presence that has been a hallmark of much of the 20th century and that has contributed to peace, stability, and prosperity in the region. To counteract this uncertainty, the administration continues to ensure that the Pacific piece of the rebalance to the Asia-Pacific is not forgotten. The United States has always been a friend and partner to the Pacific Islands, providing the region with significant levels of foreign assistance. Under the rebalance, we have stepped up our level of engagement, including expanding our staffing and programming and increasing the frequency of high-level meetings with the Pacific Island leaders.

In 2011, President Obama met with Pacific Island leaders on the margins of APEC, and in 2015, he met with the leaders of the Marshall Islands, Kiribati and Papua New Guinea at the COP-21 climate meetings in Paris. In 2012, Secretary Clinton became the first Secretary of State to attend the Pacific Islands Forum, the key policy body of the region. Since then, we have continued to engage Pacific Island leaders at high levels through the annual Pacific Islands Forum leaders' forum, most recently with the visit of Deputy Secretary of State Heather Higginbottom to the forum in 2015.

U.S. engagement at the Pacific Island Forum provides an opportunity to press issues of concern with Pacific Island leaders and for the U.S. to be responsive to the region's needs for assistance and economic development. The Pacific continues to look to the United States for leadership and support, including on fostering sustainable economic development, enhancing maritime security and combating climate change. The United States has provided over $350 million in Fiscal Year 2014 in its engagements with the region through 15 U.S. departments and agencies.

U.S. assistance includes $21 million annually provided to the Pacific Island parties to the U.S.-South Pacific Tuna Treaty. As we speak, the United States is in active negotiations over the future of this nearly 30-year-old treaty. As we deepen our longstanding engagement with the region, the United States partners closely with Australia and New Zealand, which like us, share a strong interest in ensuring the peace and prosperity of our Pacific neighbors. In recognition of the leading role Australia and New Zealand play in the Pacific, we frequently consult with them on our strategic and development issues. And we work to ensure our assistance to the region is complementary, advances our common objectives to promote sustainable and inclusive development.

While Australia and New Zealand frequently play a lead assistance role in the South Pacific, the United States and the countries of the North Pacific share especially close relationships. In particular, the Freely Associated States of the Republic of Palau, the Republic of the Marshall Islands, and the Federated States of Micronesia are an important component of the U.S. position in the Pacific. Through our respective Compacts of Free Association, the United States has maintained extraordinarily close relations with the FAS. In Fiscal Year 2014, we provided over $200 million in assistance primarily administered by the Department of the Interior to support their governance and economic advancement.

In the United Nations, the FAS have some of the highest voting coincidence with the United States. For example, in 2014, Palau had the second highest voting coincidence with the United States. Despite an increase in assistance from others interested in enhancing their engagement with the region, Palau has not only supported the United States on Israel- and Cuba-related votes but has been at the forefront of actively helping garner support of others.

Palau has supported U.N. resolutions seeking to combat the spread of weapons of mass destruction and joined in efforts to address systemic human rights abuses in North Korea, Syria and Iran.

Our relationship with not only Palau but with other FAS states allows the United States to guard its long-term defense and strategic interest in the region. We have full authority and responsibility for security and defense matters in and relating to each of the FAS, and we have the right of denial of third-country military access to them. Admissible FAS citizens have the right to work and live in the United States as non-immigrant residents. While the FAS does not maintain their own military forces, their citizens are eligible to serve in the U.S. Armed Forces. Citizens of FSM, RMI, and Palau volunteer to serve in the U.S. military at high rates, and we are grateful for their sacrifices and dedication to promoting peace worldwide.

In February, I accompanied Assistant Secretary Russel, U.S. Pacific Fleet Commander Admiral Swift, and U.S. Coast Guard District 14 Commander Rear Admiral Atkins to several Pacific Islands. One of the countries we visited was Palau. As Assistant Secretary Russel said, our commitment to the development and self-determination of the people of Palau will always endure because it is built on common history and values. We are united by the sacrifices of the thousands of Marines and other U.S. servicemembers who were killed or wounded liberating Palau during World War II, and we appreciate the Palauans who serve in the U.S. Armed Forces today.

The original process that led to our compact with Palau and the subsequent review was based on a solemn promise to help them achieve self-governance and long-term economic advancement. The assistance package within the agreement as set forth in the administration's February legislative proposal is designed to reduce

Palau's dependence on U.S. direct economic assistance as it continues to grow and reform its economy.

In addition to U.S. assistance, the terms of the agreement commit Palau to a range of economic reforms designed to help increase fiscal transparency, sustain progress achieved under compact funding, and create a stronger foundation for economic self-sufficiency. After nearly 6 years and multiple endeavors by the administration and Congress, we have as yet been unable to secure the funding necessary to bring the Compact Review Agreement into force. But bringing the agreement into force will demonstrate to Palau and our partners across the region that our commitments are not empty promises.

Mr. Chairman, in conclusion, I wish to reiterate the Pacific region's strategic importance to the United States. Our identity as a Pacific power was affirmed on the beaches of the Pacific during World War II. And since that time we have built positive and multifaceted partnerships with these countries. Our engagement in this region is about our long-term strategic interests. We will continue to work constructively with our partners in the region to maintain peace and foster sustainable, inclusive development. But we will also need the support of Congress, not only to secure funding for the Palau Compact but also to continue to support our engagement efforts across the Pacific. Thank you for the opportunity to testify before this committee.

[The prepared statement of Mr. Matthews follows:]

Statement of

Matthew Matthews
Deputy Assistant Secretary of State and Senior Official for APEC
Bureau of East Asian and Pacific Affairs
U.S. Department of State

Before the

House Foreign Affairs Committee
Subcommittee on Asia and the Pacific

June 23, 2016

Mr. Chairman, Ranking Member Sherman, and members of the Subcommittee, thank you for the opportunity to testify on U.S. policy toward Pacific island countries, and for your leadership on these issues.

The Pacific island region has been free of great power conflict since the end of World War II, and we have enjoyed friendly relations with all of the Pacific island countries. This state of affairs, however, is not guaranteed. Our partnerships and engagement in the region matter greatly.

We cooperate closely with the Pacific island countries on a wide range of globally important issues, from promoting human rights and engaging in peacekeeping operations to combating climate change and illegal, unreported, and unregulated fishing. The Pacific islanders have outsized influence on the global stage and the United States must continue to encourage them through our support for their sustainable and inclusive development.

However, it is equally important that we do not take Pacific goodwill for granted. Our relations with our Pacific partners are unfolding against the backdrop of a shifting strategic environment, where emerging powers in Asia and elsewhere seek to exert a greater influence in the Pacific region, through development and economic aid, people-to-people contacts, diplomatic engagement, and security cooperation. There is continued uncertainty in the region about the United States' willingness and ability to sustain our robust forward presence that has been a hallmark of much of the 20th century and that has contributed to peace, stability, and prosperity in the region.

To counteract this uncertainty, the Administration continues to ensure that the "Pacific" piece of the rebalance to the Asia-Pacific is not forgotten. The United States has always been a friend and partner to the Pacific islands, providing the region with significant levels of foreign assistance. Under the Rebalance, we have increased our level of engagement, including expanding our staffing and programming and increasing the frequency of high level meetings with Pacific leaders. In 2011, President Obama met with Pacific island leaders on the margins of the Asia Pacific Economic Cooperation (APEC) Forum, and in 2015 met with the leaders of the Marshall Islands, Kiribati, and Papua New Guinea at the COP-21, also known as the 2015 Paris Climate Conference. In 2012 Secretary Clinton became the first Secretary of State to attend the Pacific Islands Forum (PIF), the key policy body in the region. Since then we have continued to engage Pacific island leaders at high levels through the annual PIF Leaders' Forum, most recently with the visit of Deputy Secretary of State Heather Higginbottom to the Forum in 2015. U.S. engagement at PIF provides an opportunity to press issues of key concern with Pacific island leaders and for the U.S. to be responsive to the region's needs.

U.S. Assistance to the Pacific Islands

The Pacific continues to look to the United States for leadership and support, including on combatting climate change, enhancing maritime security, and fostering sustainable economic development. The United States has provided over $350 million in Fiscal Year 2014 in its engagement with the region through 15 U.S. departments and agencies which directly benefit the 9 million people living in the Pacific islands.

U.S. assistance includes $21 million provided annually to the Pacific island parties to the U.S.-South Pacific Tuna Treaty. As we speak, the United States is in active negotiations over the future of this nearly 30 year-old treaty.

Commercial fishing revenues are the lifeblood of Pacific Island economies, and Pacific islands struggle to patrol their over 16 million square miles of exclusive economic zones—which presents security as well as economic risks. For this reason, we work closely with these "Large Ocean States" to combat illegal, unreported, and unregulated (IUU) fishing and to build and expand maritime domain awareness capacity. The United States' "shiprider" agreements with nine Pacific Islands (Palau, Federated States of Micronesia, Republic of the Marshall Islands, Cook Islands, Kiribati, Tonga, Nauru, Tuvalu, and Samoa) provide a critical mechanism for combatting IUU fishing and enhancing maritime law enforcement cooperation. Several agreements were expanded in 2013 to include

U.S. Navy (USN) ships in addition to U.S. Coast Guard vessels and aircraft. This expansion provides additional opportunities for cooperative enforcement actions. The United States is considering pursuing new, long-term shiprider agreements with Papua New Guinea, Solomon Islands, Fiji, and Vanuatu in 2016. These agreements expand host nation maritime law enforcement capability by providing vessel platforms and U.S. Coast Guard boarding team expertise to help host nation law enforcement personnel more effectively exercise their authority and enforce their laws and regulations. The shiprider program is a cost-effective way to expand the enforcement reach of the Pacific islands. In the past six years, the U.S. Coast Guard has assisted with 203 shiprider boardings, resulting in over $4.5 million in seizures and fines.

These "large ocean states" are also highly vulnerable to natural disasters and the effects of a changing climate. Rising sea levels, for example, pose an existential threat to many of these countries. Therefore, combatting climate change is a top priority for the region and our engagement with it. We worked closely with the Pacific island countries to reach a durable, effective climate change agreement last December in Paris and many of these countries have been the first to both sign and join it (Fiji, Marshall Islands, Nauru, Palau, Samoa, and Tuvalu). The United States has also increased its support for climate change adaptation in the region. Both our assistance and our efforts to elicit significant commitments from major emitters like China and Russia on greenhouse gas reductions have been met with appreciation in the region.

History also ties the United States to the Pacific islands, especially the island hopping campaigns in the Pacific Theater during World War II. The Solomon Islands, Kiribati, the Marshall Islands, Palau, and Papua New Guinea are places where thousands of American military personnel died in action. The Defense POW/MIA Accounting Agency is still in the Pacific working in close coordination with local authorities to locate, identify, and repatriate missing American service personnel.

Another legacy of the war is unexploded ordnance (UXO), which still poses a threat to Pacific islanders more than 70 years after the cessation of conflict. In response, we have provided funding for clearing legacy ordnance, providing mine risk education and victim assistance, building local capacity to mitigate the threat, and reducing small arms / light weapons (SA/LW) proliferation. We have significant programs in the Marshall Islands, Solomon Islands, and Palau. In the Solomon Islands, in 2015, our implementing partner Golden West continued Explosive Ordnance Device (EOD) training for members of the Royal Solomon Islands Police Force (RSIPF) to improve their ability to deal with UXO. We are building the RSIPF into a regional UXO leader that can share its expertise and experience with other island nations, such as the Marshall Islands, transforming them from an assistance recipient into an assistance provider.

Partnering in the Pacific

As we deepen our longstanding engagement with the region, the United States partners closely with Australia and New Zealand, which like us, share a strong interest in ensuring the peace and prosperity of our Pacific neighbors. We also work to coordinate aid, infrastructure development, and economic development assistance with other countries active in the region, such as Japan and France as well as the European Union, World Bank, Asian Development Bank, World Health Organization, and others. In recognition of the leading role Australia and New Zealand play in the Pacific, we frequently consult with them on strategic and development issues, and we work to ensure our assistance to the region is complementary and advances our common objectives to promote sustainable and inclusive development. For instance, Australia helps promote maritime domain awareness with its Pacific Patrol Boat program which entails providing patrol boats as well as technical advisors to Pacific island countries to patrol their exclusive economic zones. Australia works closely with the U.S. Coast Guard on training in the North Pacific. On disaster relief, the United States, Australia, New Zealand and France coordinate closely both before and after disaster strikes to ensure that we are meeting the needs of affected countries but not duplicating efforts, which is key in a post-disaster environment. For example, Australia and New Zealand took the lead this year in providing humanitarian assistance and disaster recovery efforts to Fiji after one of the strongest ever recorded storms, Cyclone Winston, caused devastation and destruction across a large part of the country. When Typhoon Maysak caused extensive damage in the Federated States of Micronesia in 2015, and when drought resulting from El Nino devastated food crops and reduced the availability of potable water in the Marshall Islands in 2016, the United States issued a Presidential Disaster Declaration and USAID's Office of U.S. Foreign Disaster Assistance and the Federal Emergency Management Agency coordinated to provide assistance.

Freely Associated States

While Australia and New Zealand frequently play a lead assistance role in the South Pacific, the United States and the countries of the North Pacific share especially close relationships. These three countries in the Northern Pacific, the Republic of Palau, the Republic of the Marshall Islands (RMI), and the Federated States of Micronesia (FSM), share a special compact relationship with the United

States and are collectively referred to as The Freely Associated States (FAS). Our relationship with the FAS is a strategic component of our position in the Pacific. These relationships allow the United States to guard its long-term defense and strategic interests in the region. We have full authority and responsibility for the security and defense matters in and relating to each of the FAS and have the right of denial of third-country military access to them. In addition, all three FAS shall refrain from actions that are determined to be incompatible with our authority and responsibility for security and defense matters in or relating to the FAS. While the FAS do not maintain their own military forces, their citizens are eligible to serve in the U.S. Armed Forces. Citizens of FSM, RMI, and Palau volunteer to serve in the U.S. military at rates higher than many U.S. states, and we are grateful for their sacrifices and dedication to promoting peace worldwide. But the importance of our strong relationship with the FAS extends beyond defense considerations.

Through our respective Compacts of Free Association, the United States has maintained extraordinarily close relations with the FAS. In Fiscal Year 2014, we provided over $200 million in assistance, primarily administered by the Department of the Interior, to support their governance and economic advancement. In the United Nations, the FAS have some of the highest voting coincidences with the United States. For example, in 2014 at the 69th General Assembly Palau had the second highest voting coincidence with the United States at 90 percent. This is markedly higher than several of our closest allies including the United Kingdom (79 percent), Australia (75 percent), South Korea (67 percent), and Japan (63 percent). Despite an increase in assistance from others interested in enhancing their engagement with the region, Palau has not only supported the United States on key Israel- and Cuba-related votes but has been at the forefront of actively helping garner the support of others. The FAS have supported UN resolutions seeking to combat the spread of weapons of mass destruction, and joined in efforts to address systematic human rights abuses in North Korea, Syria, and Iran.

Admissible FAS citizens have the right to work and live in the United States as nonimmigrant residents. In fact, the Census Bureau estimated in 2011 that one fourth of all FAS citizens currently reside in the United States. It is these people-to-people ties which form the foundation for our relationships across the Pacific. Our robust Peace Corps programs in the Federated States of Micronesia, Palau, Fiji, Samoa, Tonga, and Vanuatu, comprise approximately 260 current volunteers. Indeed, the Federated States of Micronesia is home to one of the oldest Peace Corps programs globally and is celebrating its 50th anniversary this year.

Our Commitment to Palau

In February, I accompanied Assistant Secretary Russel, U.S. Pacific Fleet Commander Admiral Swift, and U.S. Coast Guard District 14 Commander Rear Admiral Atkins to several countries in the Pacific. One of the countries we visited was Palau. As Assistant Secretary Russel said, our commitment to the development and self-determination of the people of Palau will always endure – because it is built on common history and values. We are united by the sacrifices of the thousands of Marines and other U.S. service members who were killed or wounded liberating Peleliu during World War II and the 100 Palauans who serve in the U.S. Armed Forces today.

The original process that led to our Compact with Palau and the subsequent review was based on a solemn promise to help them achieve self-governance and long-term economic advancement.

The assistance package within the Agreement, as set forth in the Administration's February legislative proposal, is designed to reduce Palau's dependence on U.S. direct economic assistance as it continues to grow and reform its economy. In addition to U.S. assistance, the terms of the agreement also commit Palau to a range of economic reforms designed to help increase fiscal transparency, sustain progress achieved under Compact funding, and create a stronger foundation for economic self-sufficiency. If the bilateral Agreement between our two countries is not brought into force, the Trust Fund would be unable to provide an average annual distribution of $15 million per year until 2044, which, under the Compact as negotiated in the 1980s, has been the objective of the Trust Fund from the time it was originally established.

After nearly six years and multiple endeavors by the Administration and Congress, we have as of yet been unable to secure the funding necessary to bring the Compact Review Agreement into force. Bringing the Agreement into force will demonstrate to Palau and our partners across the region that our commitments are not empty promises.

United States: A Pacific Power

Mr. Chairman, in conclusion, I wish to reiterate the Pacific region's strategic importance to the United States. Our identity as a "Pacific power" was affirmed on the beaches of the Pacific during World War II, and since that time we have built positive, multifaceted partnerships with these countries. Our engagement in this region is about our long-term strategic interests. We will continue to work constructively with our partners in the region to maintain peace and foster sustainable, inclusive development, but we also need the support of Congress not only to secure funding for the Palau Compact Review Agreement but also to sustain our engagement across the Pacific. Thank you for the opportunity to testify before this Subcommittee.

———————

Mr. SALMON. Thank you, Mr. Matthews.
The Chair recognizes Ms. Steele.

STATEMENT OF MS. GLORIA STEELE, SENIOR DEPUTY ASSISTANT ADMINISTRATOR, BUREAU FOR ASIA, U.S. AGENCY FOR INTERNATIONAL DEVELOPMENT

Ms. STEELE. Chairman Salmon, Ranking Member Sherman, members of the subcommittee, thank you for the opportunity to testify on USAID's role in advancing U.S. foreign policy interests, including the Asia-Pacific rebalance in the Pacific Islands. The Pacific Island nations may appear as tiny and scattered dots on the globe, but they are as central to global security today as they were during the Second World War. Their strategic position in the Asia-Pacific make them more vital than ever to the global economy. A vast proportion of the world's shipping passes through Pacific waters on which millions of people depend for food and income. Many of these nations, however, are threatened as never before by the depletion of their natural resources by health threats such as HIV, TB, and the Zika virus, and especially by natural disasters. While typhoons and cyclones have long plagued the region, they are becoming more frequent and more intense.

Rising seas threaten the very existence of low-lying nations such as the Marshall Islands, the Tuvalu, and Kiribati. Ocean acidification and rising sea temperatures are damaging coral reefs and fisheries, posing major threats to food security. At USAID, our mission is to end extreme poverty and promote resilient democratic societies while advancing security and prosperity of the United States. Key to achieving success in the Pacific Islands is helping nations cope with the changing environmental conditions. Our development assistance across 12 Pacific Island nations helps people improve their lives while building a more sustainable, equitable future for all.

Next, I will provide brief overviews of our primary assistance areas. First, on adapting to changes in climatic conditions: The people of the Pacific Islands depend primarily on tourism, fisheries, forestry, and agriculture for their livelihoods, all of which are highly sensitive to changing climatic conditions. In 2015, we supported over 280 communities across 12 Pacific Island nations to mitigate the negative impacts of natural disasters. With an emphasis on women's participation, we are also providing grants and training civil society organizations to help communities adapt to changing climate while also addressing related community needs such as improving livelihood and food security. At the same time, USAID is focused on increasing regional cooperation and coordination on climate change and on strengthening intra- and intergovernmental capacity at the national level to address issues related to climate change. When disasters do occur, USAID delivers humanitarian assistance to help with basic needs. For example, in response to the drought in the Marshall Islands, which is affecting nearly 40 percent of the population, we are helping to provide supplemental food assistance, hygiene supplies, and safe drinking water. In the Marshall Islands and in Federated States of Micronesia, we also assist in post-disaster reconstruction. To help reduce the need for disaster assistance in the first place, we support communities in effectively preparing for, responding to, and mitigating the impacts of natural disasters. Assistance includes programs to develop early warning systems, train volunteers on first aid, and climate-proof water sources and community infrastructures.

On fisheries, it is estimated that more than 200 million people in the Asia-Pacific region are dependent on fisheries for food and income, yet illegal, unreported and unregulated fishing poses a major threat. In support of sustainable fisheries management, USAID is helping to develop an electronic traceability system to ensure that fish and other marine resources are legally caught and properly labeled. Currently, we are piloting this system in Indonesia and the Philippines, and once operational, we plan to expand it to other countries, including the Pacific Island nations. We are also working with the Government of Papua New Guinea on a new bilateral assistance agreement to improve sustainable management of natural resources and biodiversity. In health, we are helping to address Papua New Guinea's HIV/AIDS epidemic and related gender-based violence. We are responding to the government's recent request for assistance in addressing its multidrug-resistant TB crisis. And, finally, in democratic governance, USAID has targeted efforts to address trauma and other social issues in post-conflict Autonomous Region of Bougainville in Papua New Guinea. We are also helping to increase awareness of and preparation for its referendum on full independence that is slated to take place in 2019. USAID provided election support in Fiji during the run up to the country's 2014 elections, the first to be held since the 2006 coup.

Mr. Chairman, USAID's investments in the Pacific Islands are a critical part of the United States' vision for a peaceful, prosperous and stable Asia-Pacific. Our support for the region's sustainable inclusive development contributes to stronger U.S. diplomatic, commercial, and people-to-people relations with the Pacific Island countries, helping to advance our own security and prosperity. I appreciate the opportunity to testify today and look forward to your counsel and questions. Thank you.

[The prepared statement of Ms. Steele follows:]

Statement of Gloria Steele
Senior Deputy Assistant Administrator, Bureau for Asia
United States Agency for International Development
Before the House Committee on Foreign Affairs, Subcommittee on Asia and the Pacific
"U.S. Policy in the Pacific: The Struggle to Maintain Influence"
Thursday, June 23, 2016

Chairman Salmon, Ranking Member Sherman and Distinguished Members of the Subcommittee: Thank you for inviting me to testify on the vital role of the United States Agency for International Development (USAID) in advancing U.S. foreign policy priorities—including the Asia-Pacific Rebalance—in the Pacific islands.

On the globe, most Pacific island nations appear tiny—mere dots scattered over an area of ocean covering nearly a third of the world's surface. But these small-in-size nations are as central to global security today as they were during World War II. Their strategic position in the Asia-Pacific makes them more vital than ever to the global economy. A vast proportion of the world's shipping passes through Pacific waters, on which millions of people depend for food and income.

Many of these nations, however, are threatened as never before—by depletion of their natural resources; by health threats such as HIV/AIDS, tuberculosis and emerging diseases such as the Zika virus, which has been detected in eight of these nations; and especially by climate change. While typhoons and cyclones have long plagued the region, changes in climate have made them more frequent and intense. Last year, Super Typhoon Maysak, one of the strongest storms ever recorded, devastated the Federated States of Micronesia, and just a few months ago, Cyclone Winston, the strongest on record to hit the Southern Hemisphere, left a deadly wake in Fiji. In addition to more intense storms, rising seas threaten the very existence of low-lying nations such as the Marshall Islands, Kiribati and Tuvalu. Pacific island nations are vulnerable to sea-level rise, changing rainfall patterns and increasing drought. Further, ocean acidification and rising sea temperatures are damaging coral reefs and fisheries and consequently posing major threats to food security. Each of these impacts is expected to intensify in the coming decades.

At USAID, our mission is to end extreme poverty and promote resilient, democratic societies while advancing our security and prosperity. The key to achieving success is ensuring that development gains benefit all people—which is also critical to ensuring that development progress can be sustained over the long term. At its core, the Asia-Pacific Rebalance is about strengthening our relationships with the countries—and more specifically, with the people—of the region. USAID plays an indispensable role by helping people improve their lives and building a more sustainable, equitable future for all.

USAID's Mission in the Philippines and its Fiji-based Regional Pacific Islands Office take the lead in managing development assistance for 12 Pacific island countries: the Federated States of Micronesia, Fiji, Kiribati, Nauru, Palau, Papua New Guinea, Republic of the Marshall Islands, Samoa, Solomon Islands, Tonga, Tuvalu and Vanuatu. Our Philippines mission works closely with other USAID entities that provide assistance to the Pacific, such as the Thailand-based Regional Development Mission for Asia and the Office of U.S. Foreign Disaster Assistance (OFDA). We work with a wide range of partners—from Pacific island governments and civil society organizations (CSOs) to the private sector and Peace Corps—to ensure that USAID programs have the greatest possible impact. We coordinate our efforts closely with Australia and New Zealand, the leading donors in the region, as well as the European Union. We also coordinate programming through partnerships with regional organizations, including the three key regional Pacific organizations: the Secretariat of the Pacific Community (SPC), the Pacific Islands Forum Secretariat (PIFS) and the Secretariat of the Pacific Regional Environment Programme (SPREP).

Across all 12 Pacific island countries, USAID assistance focuses on climate change adaptation, greater disaster preparedness and providing relief when disasters do strike. In the Federated States of Micronesia and the Marshall Islands, we also assist in reconstruction from disasters. In Papua New Guinea, USAID supports biodiversity conservation and improved natural resource management, helps combat HIV/AIDS and multidrug-resistant tuberculosis, and works to strengthen democracy, peace and security in the post-conflict Autonomous Region of Bougainville. Through our regional programming, we also support sustainable fisheries management and conservation. Next, I will provide brief overviews of each of these assistance areas.

Climate Change Adaptation
The people of the Pacific islands depend primarily on tourism, fisheries, forestry and agriculture for their livelihoods—all of which are highly sensitive to changing climatic conditions. USAID is helping communities adapt to these impacts to protect lives and livelihoods in the immediate term. Since 2012, we have supported nearly 70 communities across nine Pacific island nations in making their infrastructure more resilient. This work has included drainage and flood control system upgrades, rainwater catchment system improvements, cyclone proofing of buildings, and coastal protection and erosion control projects. With an emphasis on women's participation, we are also providing grants and training to CSOs to help communities adapt to the changing climate while also addressing other community needs, such as improving livelihoods, food security or governance. For example, USAID recently supported a CSO in the Marshall Islands in expanding pearl farming as a sustainable industry for one community.

For the Pacific islands to effectively respond to the changing environmental conditions, USAID also is focused on their longer-term needs—strengthening intra- and intergovernmental capacity to successfully attract international climate adaptation financing and implement resultant programs.

In November 2015, USAID launched a five-year project in partnership with SPC, PIFS and SPREP to strengthen regional cooperation and coordination among the Pacific island countries on climate change. This project will also help strengthen their ability to successfully apply for and effectively utilize climate financing by improving systems and introducing necessary tools at the national level. We are also poised to launch another project this fall that will assist all 12 Pacific island countries in matching their needs with available financing while also updating their legal frameworks to improve implementation of adaptation strategies. This project builds on our success since 2011 helping facilitate seven projects that have mobilized more than $263 million in financing in Samoa, Solomon Islands, Tonga, Tuvalu and Vanuatu.

Emergency Response, Disaster Preparedness and Reconstruction

Across the Pacific when natural disasters occur, USAID delivers humanitarian assistance, which includes food, emergency shelter materials, safe drinking water and hygiene kits. Drought has been a particular challenge since the onset of the climatic phenomenon known as El Niño. For example, in response to a severe drought in Palau that reached a crisis point in April, USAID has responded with support for the International Organization for Migration to aid vulnerable communities. In Papua New Guinea, drought following El Niño-related frost has exacerbated flooding from seasonal rains. USAID responded with emergency and other assistance, in addition to refocusing our existing disaster risk reduction programs to directly address El Niño effects in the country.

To help reduce the need for humanitarian assistance in response to disasters, and complementing USAID's climate change adaptation assistance, we also support communities across the Pacific in effectively preparing for, responding to and mitigating the impacts of natural disasters. Accordingly, OFDA has worked in the Pacific islands for more than a decade to strengthen disaster preparedness and response. In FY 2016 alone, USAID provided nearly $10 million in disaster risk reduction programming to the Pacific islands. These programs improved hazard monitoring and early warning systems, engaged students in disaster preparedness efforts and drills, trained community volunteers on basic disaster response like first aid, prepositioned emergency relief supplies, and helped communities develop hazard maps and disaster plans. Our assistance has made a difference. For example, USAID disaster risk reduction investments in Vanuatu enabled communities to prepare in advance of Cyclone Pam in early 2015, which significantly contributed to avoiding loss of life.

In the North Pacific, under the Compacts of Free Association, as amended, between the United States and the Federated States of Micronesia and the United States and Republic of the Marshall Islands, USAID provides supplemental disaster and reconstruction assistance to the two countries. This assistance includes prepositioning humanitarian relief supplies in warehouses from where assistance can be mobilized quickly in times of need, developing and improving disaster response and reconstruction plans, and training government employees and civil society representatives in disaster response best practices. Our support under the compacts includes reconstruction efforts in the wake of natural disasters following a Presidential Disaster Declaration (PDD). The Federal Emergency Management Agency (FEMA) covers USAID's costs in cases when a PDD is issued. For example, through the FEMA-funded $30 million Typhoon Maysak Reconstruction Program, USAID is helping Micronesian communities rebuild after last year's super typhoon.

Fisheries and Biodiversity Conservation

It is estimated that over 200 million people in the Asia-Pacific are directly or indirectly dependent on fisheries for food and income. Yet illegal, unreported and unregulated fishing is one of the major identified threats to fisheries in the Coral Triangle region, which spans six Southeast Asian and Pacific countries and contains one of the greatest concentrations of marine biodiversity in the world. This illegal fishing can also play a major role in fueling human trafficking in the region.

In support of regional, sustainable fisheries management, USAID is helping to develop an electronic traceability system to ensure that fish and other marine resources are legally caught and properly labeled. Currently, we are piloting this system in Indonesia and the Philippines, and once it is operational, we have plans to expand it to other countries, including island nations in the Pacific. In announcing the USAID Oceans and Fisheries Partnership (known as USAID Oceans) in August 2015, Secretary of State John Kerry said, "Traceability is an essential part of our global fight to conserve marine resources and protect the health of our oceans."

As part of USAID's overall assistance to the six-nation Coral Triangle Initiative on Coral Reefs, Fisheries and Food Security, USAID supported the development and use of a mobile phone app in the Solomon Islands to manage the country's inshore fisheries. Without precise and centralized data, fisheries management had previously proven difficult in this geographically dispersed island country. Paper entries were sometimes wet and illegible and data were not entered into a consolidated database to support management decisions. But with the mobile phone app, surveyors are now able to take stock each day of fish arriving by canoes and boats at local markets and feed this information into a database that gives government and the fishing industry vital information needed to manage fisheries.

Papua New Guinea, one of the countries in the Coral Triangle area, is home to more than 5 percent of the world's biodiversity, with the country's forests representing the third largest expanse of tropical rainforest in the world. Papua New Guinea's biodiversity, however, is also among the world's most threatened. USAID has identified Papua New Guinea as one of the Agency's priority countries for assistance in biodiversity conservation. USAID is working with the Government of Papua New Guinea on a new bilateral assistance agreement to improve capacity to manage natural resources sustainably and conserve the country's rich and unique biodiversity.

Combating Infectious Diseases in Papua New Guinea
Papua New Guinea is the most populous of the Pacific island nations and suffers from one of the highest rates of HIV/AIDS in the region. While overall adult prevalence is nearly 1 percent, HIV infection rates are much higher among key populations, including female sex workers and men who have sex with men. Poor surveillance and lack of capacity at all levels exacerbate the enormous challenge HIV/AIDS poses to the nation's already weak health system.

USAID addresses Papua New Guinea's HIV/AIDS epidemic by working with the national government to link and strengthen prevention, care, support and treatment services for key populations. Our focus is on ensuring key populations are initiated into treatment and retained. We also work with those affected by gender-based violence, a key contributing factor to HIV infection in women. USAID-supported HIV prevention, care and treatment sites have served nearly 5,000 people in Papua New Guinea. We have also provided nearly 750 clients with dedicated antiretroviral therapy nurses. This strong, supportive approach to case management has paid off; the patient adherence rate for USAID-supported clinics is over 75 percent.

In addition, USAID is supporting the Government of Papua New Guinea's recent request for assistance in strengthening its response to the country's multidrug-resistant tuberculosis (MDR-TB) crisis. Controlling the highly infectious, airborne disease is especially critical in light of the country's increasing role in hosting international events. Last year, Papua New Guinea hosted the Pacific Games, and in 2018, the country is slated to host the Asia-Pacific Economic Cooperation leaders' summit for the first time. USAID is providing targeted technical assistance to help detect and treat drug-resistant TB strains, which includes providing two GeneXpert machines, American technology that diagnoses MDR-TB in hours instead of weeks. We are also partnering to bring the first TB drug on the market in more than 40 years—called bedaquiline— to Papua New Guinea to battle strains resistant to the most effective drugs available today.

Targeted Democracy Initiatives
In the Autonomous Region of Bougainville in Papua New Guinea, USAID is helping the community achieve sustainable peace, security and development. The decade-long conflict that began in 1989 displaced more than half the population and took the lives of up to 20,000 people, leaving families and communities across Bougainville struggling with many issues that impede reconciliation, rehabilitation and development, including trauma, domestic violence and substance abuse. Over the past two years, USAID worked with women's CSOs to raise awareness of and strengthen services in mental health, trauma counseling and gender-based violence. Our assistance improved mental health services in 15 rural clinics across Bougainville and provided trauma counseling to more than 1,800 individuals. We also helped deepen public knowledge and commitment to addressing post-conflict issues through radio messages and workshops reaching more than 390,000 people.

In addition, during the months leading up to Bougainville's May 2015 general elections and continuing today, USAID has helped to increase awareness of and preparation for the upcoming referendum on full independence from Papua New Guinea that is slated to take place in 2019.

USAID also provided elections support in Fiji during the run-up to the country's 2014 national elections—the first to be held since a 2006 coup. In the weeks and months leading up to the election, where nearly half of those who cast ballots were first-time voters, USAID's Elections and Political Processes Fund supported the dissemination of voter education information to more than 260,000 Fijians. USAID also trained civil society leaders and parliamentarians to engage on policy issues in a town hall format, which led to the country's first town hall meeting in January 2015 with newly-elected parliament members.

Conclusion
Mr. Chairman, USAID's investments in the Pacific islands region are a critical part of the United States' vision for a peaceful, prosperous and stable Asia-Pacific. By addressing the root causes of poverty, conflict and instability, development plays an indispensable role alongside defense and diplomacy in advancing our strategic interests. Our support for the region's sustainable and inclusive development contributes to stronger U.S. diplomatic, commercial and people-to-people relations with the Pacific island countries, helping to advance our own security and prosperity.

Thank you for the opportunity to share with you what USAID is doing in this important region of the world. I look forward to your counsel and questions.

###

_____

Mr. SALMON. Thank you.

The Chair recognizes Mr. Sherman.

Mr. SHERMAN. Thank you, Mr. Chairman, for a chance to deliver an opening statement. We had a markup and a hearing scheduled at various times, and I am glad that we have started this hearing.

I want to thank you for holding this hearing on countries with 9 million people living in a dozen countries. These islands, as has been noted, play an important role in U.S. history over the last 75 years, particularly during World War II. I believe these islands will be more important this century than perhaps they were last century because they, you know—I want to get testimony on this from our witnesses—they control an enormous amount of economic zone ocean floor and fish resources. The ability of our species to exploit the ocean and its floor are going to increase. Our need for natural resources is going to increase. And 200 miles around every inhabited island adds up to a tremendous portion of the Pacific.

I will also be asking our witnesses, and they may or may not know this, whether an island that has previously been uninhabited acquires a 200-mile radius economic zone when one family chooses to live there. Many of these islands, as noted, were important in World War II. They were important during the cold war, and we get support from most of these countries when issues come before the United Nations.

The Compact of Free Association that we have with Micronesia, the Marshall Islands and Palau, represent our recognition of our international partnership with these countries over the years and our joint interests. One issue that needs particular attention is the Palau Compact review. This agreement was designed to help people of Palau achieve self-governance and economic self-sufficiency. The United States should abide by its commitments. I know we have had difficulty securing the funds necessary to bring the Palau Compact review fully into force, and I look forward to working with the administration and our colleagues to achieve that.

As to climate change, the nations of the Pacific are the most vulnerable, along with the other island nations in the Indian and Atlantic Oceans, to climate change. Climate change is already impacting the everyday lives of residents through sea level rise, more frequent storms, et cetera. Assistance in responding to these impacts often constitutes a large part of our aid and our other relations with Pacific Island countries. Extreme climate events have also impacted water, coastal, and marine resources and agriculture. I will point out that there are some on the right who will say we shouldn't talk about this because there couldn't be any global warming, and then there are some on the left who say you cannot talk about remediating or preparing for global warming either because you should not admit that that is a possible thing to do or because anything that diminishes the harm of global warming diminishes our incentive to deal with it. The fact is we need to be practical. There is global warming. We will not fully stop it in the decade to come, and helping our friends of the Pacific deal with it is one of the best uses of our USAID budget.

I would like to hear specific details from USAID of efforts to help these countries deal with critical climate affected needs. What programs have worked and what countries have been most capable of working with us?

Finally, I want to address a legal matter involving Tonga. Two families in the San Fernando Valley were among the victims of an investment fraud scheme where the alleged fraudster absconded to Tonga. For the past several years, efforts to extradite him to face trial in the Central District of California, where he has been indicted, have moved, shall we say, slowly through the Tongan courts. A lower Tongan court recently determined that the U.S. Tongan fraud laws were too dissimilar to warrant extradition under the treaty, a decision that appears highly questionable.

The application of dual criminality that is at the extradition law concept—the alleged criminal activity must be a crime in both countries in order for it to be an extraditable offense—has been applied, but it should be applied to lead to extradition. In this fraud matter, it would be a violation if—and obviously, the defendant has not been convicted—but the crimes set forth in the indictment would constitute a crime in every country of the world that maintains as reasonable rule of law system. So now that decision is being appealed by the Tongan Government with the expectation that the appeal will be heard in September. And I for one will be looking to see whether the rule of law and reasonable decision-making is taking place in Tonga.

The life savings of my constituents were wiped out. There is an indictment of an American suspected of having defrauded them and others. The activities for which the individual is wanted in the United States would be a crime in every country, and he ought to be extradited as soon as possible. And keep in mind, this is an American suspect. There is no argument that somehow a Tongan is going to be discriminated against in the United States court system.

I urge the State and Justice Departments to work closely, and I know our witnesses, whether they choose to comment on this case right now, I know that the State Department will be focused on this.

I yield back.

Mr. SALMON. We will now go to the questions.

I would like to ask the first question. The U.S. still hasn't completed a long-term solution to the Tuna Treaty stalemate. Voices within the U.S. tuna industry continue to view the treaty as obsolete, irresponsive to market conditions, and economically unfeasible. How would the U.S.' withdrawal from the South Pacific Tuna Treaty affect the diplomatic relationships between the United States and the Forum Fisheries Agency member countries, Mr. Matthews?

Mr. MATTHEWS. Mr. Chairman, if in fact it comes to the point where there is no way to bridge differences over the key elements of extending the Tuna Treaty and we do, in fact, complete withdrawal, I believe that the United States' relationship with Pacific Island nations are sufficiently broad and deep that we can find ways to sustain our close cooperation and the important relationships that we have today. I believe there are many ways in which we are providing assistance and development aid, that our cooperation on capacity building and in areas of security will continue.

That said, the Tuna Treaty and the work that has been done under it has been very helpful in maintaining our position, so we do continue, even as we speak, to work during a fifth round of negotiations that are currently being conducted in Auckland in hopes that some workable path forward can be found.

Mr. SALMON. Thank you very much.

My next question is regarding Taiwan. And, Mr. Matthews, you were just there so maybe it would be appropriate. It would probably be appropriate for either one of you, but of the 22 nations that maintain full diplomatic relations with Taiwan, six are Pacific Islands region: Kiribati, the Marshall Islands, Nauru, Palau, and Solomon Islands and Tuvalu. With tension between President Tsai's new administration and the government in Beijing, some experts are worrying about a return to dollar diplomacy and efforts to change recognition ending a multiyear truce. Are we concerned about such efforts in the Pacific? Are we taking steps to encourage countries in the Pacific to maintain the status quo? Would you like to take a first stab, Mr. Matthews?

And, Ms. Steele, I would love to hear you thoughts, if you have any, on that.

Mr. MATTHEWS. Thank you, Mr. Chairman.

Ms. STEELE. No, I would defer to my colleague on this.

Mr. MATTHEWS. The United States has a longstanding policy of supporting the maintenance of international space for Taiwan. We do that through a number of different venues. Of course, we support Taiwan's participation in any international organization that does not require sovereignty. And those organizations that do require sovereignty, we still seek meaningful participation for Taiwan, and we also have additional venues for helping Taiwan maintain international space, and that includes a cooperation framework that I participated in just a few days ago in Taiwan, the Global Cooperation Training Framework, where we work together with Taiwan to bring international players to Taiwan where Taiwan's expertise and the United States' expertise can be used jointly to help promote development and dissemination of important knowledge. That last session that we had was on energy efficiency, and it not only had participation from India and Southeast Asia, but also from Pacific Island nations.

So I think there are a number of venues by which we are able to assure that Taiwan does have international space. I won't say that there is not any concern that there might be some, you know, future stress placed on their international space, but it is clear that the United States is there to help support and maintain it.

Mr. SALMON. I thank the gentleman.

I am going to recognize Mr. Bera.

Mr. BERA. Thank you, Chairman Salmon, and thank the witnesses.

You know, let me ask my first question.

Ms. Steele, as, you know, the administration pivots to Asia, you know, we often talk about China, Japan, Korea, South Asia, you know. With regards to the pivot to Asia and the Pacific Islands, specifically, you know, could you give us how the administration is viewing the potential for Pacific Islands and what their focus there is?

Ms. STEELE. Thank you, Mr. Bera. Just as soon as then Secretary Clinton announced the pivot to Asia, within a month, we opened up a USAID satellite office in Papua New Guinea, and within 6 months, we started implementing climate change programs. These are very important to the people of the Pacific, as I have mentioned earlier. They are among the most disaster-prone countries in the world, and we are helping to mitigate the impact of the natural disasters and helping them to be prepared for those impacts.

And in Papua New Guinea itself, we have set up programs to address HIV/AIDS and TB. They are suffering from multidrug-resistant TB right now and the related gender-based violence in those countries. And in the runup to the elections in Fiji, we also provided assistance, which has resulted in contributing to the drafting of their Constitution of 2013 and a very successful election in 2014, the first one since 2006.

Mr. BERA. Great, thank you, Ms. Steele.

Either Mr. Matthews or Ms. Steele, you know, the ranking member touched on climate change. He touched on preparations for climate change. If you were to quantify, you know, how big a threat climate change and rising oceans is going to be and then also how the islands are preparing. I don't know if you want to start, Mr. Matthews, or——

Mr. MATTHEWS. Well, I think it is commonly recognized that particularly Pacific Island nations that are atoll nations and who have very little space to deal with in terms of the high points above sea level—some nations have a maximum of 3 meters above sea level is their highest point. And these Pacific Islands, like the Marshall Islands, like Kiribati, are particularly vulnerable. They are vulnerable to the potential impacts of sea rise, but they are vulnerable already to major climatic storms and sea surges, and they already suffer problems and do, in fact, require remediation. As Congressman Sherman mentioned, remediation is a necessary aspect of the work we do with them, and we are, in fact, already engaged in a number of programs. But we are also, under the new Paris Agreement, going to be ensuring that we provide access for Pacific Island nations to funding that will be a part of the global fund, and we are actually initiating programs to help them learn how to go about doing that and to do it effectively and efficiently.

Ms. STEELE. If I may add, Mr. Bera.

Mr. BERA. Yeah.

Ms. STEELE. The Pacific Islands, as I mentioned earlier, bear a lot of the brunt of natural disasters. Just look at statistics, when we first opened their operations there, emergency assistance was at $175,000 for the entire year. Last year, in 2015, it was $13.3 million. The frequency and the intensity of the disasters have become very obvious. The strongest typhoon hit Micronesia in 2015, and then in Fiji in 2016. And so it is an issue because these countries depend largely on natural resources, tourism, fisheries, agriculture, and forestry.

Mr. BERA. In the last minute that I have, in terms of preparation to deal with sea rise and the increasing frequency of these natural disasters, what do you think it will take, and what is our timeline like?

I don't know, Ms. Steele or Mr. Matthews, whatever.

Ms. STEELE. It will take a significant amount of effort and collaboration and cooperation among the different parties involved, from the communities to civil societies to governments and regional institutions. There is a lot of work that needs to be done, measures that need to be taken at the household and the community levels, and proper planning and policymaking at the national level.

Mr. BERA. And do you see that taking place right now, the framework of that?

Ms. STEELE. Yes, Mr. Bera. All of the donors are coordinating and working very closely, leveraging each other's resources to support the different countries in the 12 Pacific Island nations.

Mr. BERA. Great. Thanks.

My time has expired. I will yield back.

Mr. SALMON. Thank you.

Mr. Sherman.

Mr. SHERMAN. Oh, you don't have a——

Mr. SALMON. We actually go to the noncommittee members after all of the members have asked their questions.

Mr. SHERMAN. Tulsi, you want to go now, or do you want me to go now?

Ms. GABBARD. Either way.

Mr. SHERMAN. Why don't we go to the gentlelady from Hawaii?

Mr. SALMON. Great. We will.

Ms. GABBARD. Thank you, Mr. Chairman, Ranking Member, thank you both for being here today.

I wanted to ask you about Vanuatu. According to a recent report from the Center for Strategic Studies' Maritime Transparency Initiative, they added Vanuatu—or Vanuatu is on the list of countries that publicly stated the South China Sea arbitral tribunal under the U.N. Convention on the Law of the Sea is illegitimate. I am wondering if you could share your thoughts on why they have taken this position and where you think other Pacific Island nations stand on the Philippines v. China tribunal case.

Mr. MATTHEWS. I believe, you know, China has been reaching out to Pacific Island nations over the past year seeking their support. I believe, to date, Vanuatu is the only Pacific Island nation that has spoken out in support of Beijing's position on the arbitral panel's future decision. The other Pacific Island nations, I believe, like us, believe that the outcome of the arbitral decision is going to be any member of the UNCLOS treaty is subject to it and that they should abide by the outcome of that.

They also believe that—and they have not agreed to China's claims to the South China Sea. Most recently, there were statements from Beijing that Fiji, in fact, had agreed to Beijing's position, and the Prime Minister Bainimarama specifically spoke out to say, no, that was not the case and that they did not take a position on among claimants and that they stood for international law applying to the resolution of those decisions.

So I think, in general, we are in a very good place. Once our new Ambassador to Vanuatu, who is resident in Port Moresby in Papua New Guinea, is able to present her credentials, she will be reaching out to the government there to engage on this issue.

Ms. GABBARD. With respect to Fiji and our relationship with Fiji, given the strain that occurred after their military coup and the democratic elections that followed, can you speak to what the status of our relationship is and, you know, kind of what you see as the path going forward, both with Fiji but also looking to see how we can strengthen our relationship with these other Pacific Island nations?

Mr. MATTHEWS. In the case of Fiji, we do, in fact, welcome the return to democracy in 2014. And since that time, we have been increasing our interaction with them, both on the diplomatic side but on the security side as well. That process will continue in a step-by-step fashion, and we are continuing to encourage the Government of Fiji to create greater space for civil society and for their opposition consistent with their commitment to democracy. And as that happens, I think you will find the pace of our relationship speeding up and strengthening.

For other Pacific Island nations, I mean, we have ongoing warm and close relationships with all Pacific Island countries, and I fully anticipate that will continue to be the case.

Ms. GABBARD. Were there any specific hard actions that were taken by the United States against Fiji or anything withheld after the military coup took place?

Mr. MATTHEWS. Well, there was a cessation of military exchanges and training, and that is beginning to come back into play as a part of the Pacific Command's general process of reengaging. And I think that is fully appreciated by the Fijians.

Ms. GABBARD. Okay. Thank you.

Thank you, Mr. Chairman.

Mr. SALMON. Thank you. Mr. Sherman, did you——

Mr. SHERMAN. No, absolutely.

The briefing materials for this hearing basically indicate that, for the area, we are providing $233 million per year in aid and elsewhere say that China may be doing $150 million, but the $150 million is really just loans similar to what our Ex-Im Bank would do; that is to say promoting their own economy by giving concessionary financing for the export of their goods and services.

If we want to compare apples to apples, aid dollars, here is money to benefit you, you get to keep, are we at 233, and what is China at?

Mr. MATTHEWS. The figures I have, Congressman, are that our total package of assistance in 2014 was actually $350 million. That is in addition to aid. There is a lot of direct government—U.S. Government agency assistance to the Pacific Islands. There are over 30 different government agencies and departments that actually do contribute. And that is real substantial assistance.

For China, I actually don't know what the split is between actual grant amounts and the actual loan amount. I would be happy to go find that information out for you and get back to you on that.

Mr. SHERMAN. Okay. The information I had included development assistance, economic support fund, global health programs, international military education and training, and regional development mission to Asia plus the South Pacific Tuna Treaty. In addition to those that did add up to 233, what are the ones that are missing from our briefing materials?

Mr. MATTHEWS. There is other assistance that is provided. The FAA provides assistance for aviation authorities in the Pacific Island states. I believe in the case of Palau, there was over $30 million provided over the past couple of years to help upgrade their airport and other associated facilities. Health and Human Services provides assistance, and I would have to go back through, but there are—it is actually pretty substantial.

Mr. SHERMAN. Good. And, yet, we still are not in compliance with the agreement with Palau.

Mr. MATTHEWS. To the extent, you know, all of the aid I have noted is really important, but as many people have already spoken up to say, if we can fulfill our obligation under the 2010 treaty to fund Palau, we will be in a far better place. It is incumbent on us to do that and the sooner——

Mr. SHERMAN. Is there any aid we are providing to Palau that doesn't qualify under the treaty and if we just gave money for this rather than for that, without increasing our total expenditures, we would be in greater—we would be closer to compliance?

Mr. MATTHEWS. I think we actually have to take this specific action to fund the agreement, and there is—the other thing I would say about this is that we want to be able to fund the agreement for the long term to actually fulfill our promise and to signal to the region that our commitment is real.

Mr. SHERMAN. Well, then, let me move on to another question. Papua New Guinea has agreed to allow the Bougainville regional government to hold a referendum on self-determination. The date could be in mid-2020 or even a target date of June 2019. Is this referendum actually likely to occur by the end of 2020? And how is it likely to turn out? Are we about to see the birth of a new nation?

Mr. MATTHEWS. Well, first of all, we really welcome Papua New Guinea's decision to move forward on this. They are obligated to do so, but now they are actually clearly signaling that they are prepared to move forward on this, and it is very possible. Well, we don't know what the outcome of that referendum vote will be, but it is possible that it would lead to the creation of a new state.

Mr. SHERMAN. What would be the population of the new state, or what is the population of the regional government's area?

Mr. MATTHEWS. Bougainville, I am not sure. It is going to be under a million in any case. The total population of Papua New Guinea is a little over 7 million.

Mr. SHERMAN. Got you.

Ms. STEELE. If I may.

Mr. SHERMAN. Yes.

Ms. STEELE. We are currently helping the Autonomous Region of Bougainville by working with their civil society, raising awareness, and getting dialogue going about the meaning of the referendum that is coming, so that they are well aware of what this means to them, what the implications are when they go and vote, if and when they go and vote.

Mr. SHERMAN. And you have a world structure that is based on a sovereign state being a much larger entity than that. I realize there are exceptions in the islands of the Pacific. I would hope that just in terms of defining what it is to be an independent sovereign state, that various regions that had a population of just a million or so could be suitably federated parts of or autonomous regions within states. When you start going to the United Nations General Assembly and meet people who represent fewer folks than I do, one wonders why the San Fernando Valley doesn't have at least one vote in the United Nations.

And I yield back.

Mr. SALMON. Thank you.

Mrs. Radewagen, did you have any questions?

Mrs. RADEWAGEN. Thank you, Mr. Chairman.

I want to thank you and the ranking member for inviting me here to be at this hearing. The Pacific Island nations are near and dear to my heart because I have lived in the Marshall Islands as well as the Northern Mariana Islands. I have been all over those islands, and so I am very understanding of the compacts, as well as the Palau Compact, which I fully support.

However, I am here today because of the importance of fishing in my home district of American Samoa. So I have a couple of questions here, Mr. Matthews. I understand that the U.S. Tuna Treaty negotiations, which are going on right now, are reaching a critical stage. I trust you realize how important the successful conclusion of these negotiations is to American Samoa. The treaty is vital for fishing access by United States vessels, many of which land their fish in American Samoa. I would appreciate assurances that the State Department is doing all it can to finalize a new treaty, which provides a viable future for the U.S. fishing fleet. And I understand that an agreement on minimum days has been reached or is close. But how companies contract for extra fishing days may be subject to Department of State approval. What is the reason for that?

Mr. MATTHEWS. First of all, I can assure you that we are making every effort possible to reach what we believe, in consultation with the U.S. fishing industry, which also includes representatives from American Samoa—they have been participants in all four rounds, and I believe they are participating now—that we will reach an agreement if we can reach a sustainable economically viable outcome. That requires understanding on fishing days, charges for fishing days, certainty of how elements under the agreement will be dealt with to make sure that the American fishing fleet gets proper clarity on what its obligations are and how those will be executed for the period of the agreement and that the agreement will be for a substantial period of time to provide the industry with a clear path forward to know how to invest, how to prepare, and to know that they will have an economically viable future.

All of these elements are critical. We certainly understand the great importance of American fishing to American Samoa and, particularly, to providing fish for the canneries that are there, and we will be making every effort to make sure we have an economically viable outcome. If we do not reach an agreement, if that does not happen, the American fishing fleet will still have the ability to negotiate with the relevant states on their own, and we will be working to make sure, though, that if there is any possible way to get to a viable outcome under the treaty itself, then that will be our first order of approach.

Mrs. RADEWAGEN. Thank you. One of the key elements of the treaty and, even more importantly, of the United States' position at the Western and Central Pacific Fisheries Commission, the other international mechanism governing U.S. fishing access in the region, is the matter of fishing on the high seas. I am sponsoring legislation intended to ensure that the WCPFC regulation of fishing by United States vessels, especially on the high seas, is science-based and establishes a level playing field relative to fishing by other flag fleets. I hope that the Department of State and other U.S. Government agencies will support this legislation.

Mr. MATTHEWS. Thank you, Congresswoman.

I just want to say that we are committed to ensuring that the U.S. Pacific fleet does, in fact, fish in a sustainable way in a manner which is consistent with laws and requirements, and we believe that their behavior over time has been exemplary. And we hope that other fishing fleets in the Pacific will follow similarly sustainable approaches.

Mrs. RADEWAGEN. Thank you, Mr. Chairman.

I yield back.

Mr. SALMON. Thank you.

The Chair now recognizes Mr. Sablan for any questions he might have.

Mr. SABLAN. Yes, thank you very much, Mr. Chairman.

Mr. Matthews and Ms. Steele, thank you very much for joining us today and also for your service to our country.

I am the only Micronesian in Congress, having been a citizen of the Trust Territory of the Pacific Islands. And growing up, of course, I heard stories about World War II. Just to set the facts straight—and this is in no way intended to disparage anyone—Guam was indeed liberated by the United States. The rest of the Pacific Islands were caught in a war between the United States and Japan, just to set the record straight.

But let me ask if—I have been on two trips to Australia and New Zealand, actually booking on flights, one with Natural Resources, and the other one with Foreign Affairs. But, Mr. Matthews, how much do we rely on Australia to form our view of what is going on in the South Pacific?

Mr. MATTHEWS. Actually, Congressman, Australia and New Zealand are both important partners for us and have extensive involvement in the South Pacific and provide a substantial amount of aid to Pacific Island nations in the South Pacific whereas we probably are the more, you know, critical partner in the North Pacific.

Mr. SABLAN. I understand, but in terms of——

Mr. MATTHEWS. In the South Pacific, they are very important partners across the board, and we do, in fact, rely on them for a lot of our understanding about what is happening there, sir.

Mr. SABLAN. Okay. And so when we are going—the difference between our treatment of Australia and New Zealand, there still remain some differences, I think, in the level of treatment. Is there any time in our foreseeable future where the Prime Minister of Australia would be welcome to the United States and I don't know what they call it—have a state dinner, maybe address a joint session of Congress? Are we getting close to that?

Mr. MATTHEWS. For Australia?

Mr. SABLAN. For New Zealand.

Mr. MATTHEWS. Oh, for New Zealand. Well, we have a very close and growing partnership with New Zealand. The relationship between President Obama and Prime Minister Key is very close, very warm. They get together on the margins of international meetings, and Prime Minister Key has, in fact, visited Washington. And so whether or not there will be a state dinner planned, I can guarantee you that this is a relationship on an upward trajectory.

Mr. SABLAN. That is what I would like to hear. I hope it continues to go upward——

Mr. MATTHEWS. It will.

Mr. SABLAN [continuing]. And what has happened in the past will, you know, eventually be water under the bridge.

Let me go back to my specific interest here. Does the administration believe that Palau is of strategic importance to the United States because of its geography and proximity to countries potentially unfriendly to the United States?

Mr. MATTHEWS. We absolutely believe that Palau has enormous strategic value, not just Palau in isolation but Palau as part of the larger Freely Associated States. They represent a vast swath of the Pacific where the United States, under the compact agreements, has specialized defense rights, and its geographical location is in fact quite critical, and it is among the various reasons that we really ought to do everything we can to fund the Palau Compact as soon as possible.

Mr. SABLAN. With no disrespect, but I am running out of time. There are 12 Pacific Island nations. And three have compacts with the United States, including Palau, of course. As for the other nine, China is trying to establish a foothold in the area. Cuba has actually established through a medical program in the Solomon Islands that relationship. Now, even Russia has engaged in Fiji. We have transfers of military equipment. The general population in the region is friendly toward the U.S., but if the U.S. does not follow through on its commitments to a compact state, that sends a bad signal to other states in the region.

And you keep saying that you continue to engage with the different countries, but continuing to have conversations when you reach an agreement and then, for 5 years, not approve that agreement, not enacted it into law, that doesn't send a good signal, does it, Mr. Matthews?

Mr. MATTHEWS. Well, I agree with you totally, Mr. Congressman. But, actually, everything has been done to put that agreement into force, except the funding.

Mr. SABLAN. Well, no, no, not everything has been done.

Mr. MATTHEWS. The funding.

Mr. SABLAN. Yeah, I don't argue whether it is a problem with helium gas or U.S. passports, the cost of U.S. passports, but for the people of Palau, they are looking to the United States and saying, what happened to the piece of document we signed, we negotiated, we agreed? Why is the issue of helium gas and passports becoming their problem?

Mr. MATTHEWS. All I can say is the sooner we can fund the agreement, the sooner it will enter into force.

Mr. SABLAN. Then why did we enter into an agreement that we couldn't fund?

Mr. MATTHEWS. I have to refer that question back to Congress. It is up to Congress to decide how to go about funding it.

Mr. SABLAN. Congress didn't sign the agreement. With no disrespect, I am just trying to iron it out.

Mr. MATTHEWS. Sure. I appreciate it.

Mr. SABLAN. Thank you very much.

Mr. MATTHEWS. Thank you.

Mr. SABLAN. Mr. Chairman, I yield.

Mr. SALMON. I thank the gentleman.

And I thank the witnesses today. It has been a great hearing. We appreciate all your hard work on behalf of the islands and the region. And I thank the ranking member for his support for this hearing today.

And, without objection, this hearing will stand adjourned.

[Whereupon, at 3:07 p.m., the subcommittee was adjourned.]

APPENDIX

MATERIAL SUBMITTED FOR THE RECORD

SUBCOMMITTEE HEARING NOTICE
COMMITTEE ON FOREIGN AFFAIRS
U.S. HOUSE OF REPRESENTATIVES
WASHINGTON, DC 20515-6128

Subcommittee on Asia and the Pacific
Matt Salmon (R-AZ), Chairman

June 23, 2016

TO: MEMBERS OF THE COMMITTEE ON FOREIGN AFFAIRS

You are respectfully requested to attend an OPEN hearing of the Committee on Foreign Affairs, to be held by the Subcommittee on Asia and the Pacific in Room 2172 of the Rayburn House Office Building (and available live on the Committee website at http://www.ForeignAffairs.house.gov):

DATE: Thursday, June 23, 2016

TIME: 2:15 p.m.

SUBJECT: U.S. Policy in the Pacific: The Struggle to Maintain Influence

WITNESSES: Mr. Matthew J. Matthews
Deputy Assistant Secretary for Australia, New Zealand, and the Pacific Islands
Senior Official for APEC
Bureau of East Asian and Pacific Affairs
U.S. Department of State

Ms. Gloria Steele
Senior Deputy Assistant Administrator
Bureau for Asia
U.S. Agency for International Development

By Direction of the Chairman

COMMITTEE ON FOREIGN AFFAIRS

MINUTES OF SUBCOMMITTEE ON _____ *Asia and the Pacific* _____ HEARING

Day___*Thursday*___Date_____*6/23/16*_____Room_____*2172*_____

Starting Time ____*2:06pm*____Ending Time ____*3:07pm*____

Recesses |____| (____to ____) (____to ____) (____to ____) (____to ____) (____to ____) (____to ____)

Presiding Member(s)

Salmon

Check all of the following that apply:

Open Session [✓]   Electronically Recorded (taped) [ ]
Executive (closed) Session [ ]   Stenographic Record [ ]
Televised [ ]

TITLE OF HEARING:

U.S. Policy in the Pacific: The Struggle to Maintain Influence

SUBCOMMITTEE MEMBERS PRESENT:

Perry
Sherman, Bera, Gabbard

NON-SUBCOMMITTEE MEMBERS PRESENT: *(Mark with an * if they are not members of full committee.)*

Radewagen
Sablan

HEARING WITNESSES: Same as meeting notice attached? Yes [✓] No [ ]
(If "no", please list below and include title, agency, department, or organization.)

STATEMENTS FOR THE RECORD: *(List any statements submitted for the record.)*

TIME SCHEDULED TO RECONVENE _____
or
TIME ADJOURNED ____*3:07pm*____

_____
Subcommittee Staff Director

MATERIAL SUBMITTED FOR THE RECORD BY THE HONORABLE MATT SALMON, A REP-
RESENTATIVE IN CONGRESS FROM THE STATE OF ARIZONA, AND CHAIRMAN, SUB-
COMMITTEE ON ASIA AND THE PACIFIC

STATEMENT OF
J. DOUGLAS HINES

HEARING ON
U.S. POLICY IN THE PACIFIC: THE STRUGGLE TO MAINTAIN INFLUENCE

JUNE 23, 2016

ASIA AND THE PACIFIC SUBCOMMITTEE
FOREIGN AFFAIRS COMMITTEE
U.S. HOUSE OF REPRESENTATIVES

My name is James Douglas Hines and I am a partner and owner of the Sea Global and Ocean Global Companies. The Global Companies own and operate 14 modern U.S. purse seine fishing vessels that are dedicated to harvesting tuna in the Central and South Pacific Ocean. Much of the tuna we harvest is cleaned near the fishing grounds and then sent to California and Georgia where it is processed and canned by two major tuna brands. Fish from our boats support thousands of U.S. jobs across America, and provide for safe, sustainable, and socially responsible fisheries products to millions of U.S. consumers.

As the Subcommittee is aware, the 38 vessels that make up the U.S. distant water tuna fleet fish under licenses issued pursuant to the South Pacific Tuna Treaty. This Treaty, originally approved by Congress in 1987, was groundbreaking in that it provided U.S. vessels access to the waters of 16 Pacific island nations. Associated with the Treaty was a separate economic assistance agreement that originally provided $10 million of economic aid annually to the participating island nations. The Treaty has served as the basis for the development of strong commercial relationship among the U.S. tuna industry and the Pacific Island nations.

The Treaty is now expired, which is why I am currently in Auckland, NZ with the U.S. delegation working to renew and extend it. The delegation is led by the State Department and NOAA with the participation of most vessel owners. Vessel owners know that unless the Treaty is renewed and restructured, the industry will be severely damaged and a number of U.S. flag boats will be sold to other countries, or simply go out of business.

We are at a critical juncture in the Pacific and this Subcommittee should be notified that unless the United States pays more attention to this part of the world, we will become insignificant players, willing to hand over our influence to China and others. Make no mistake about it, without a Treaty there will be no basis for U.S. commercial and diplomatic engagement with the Pacific Island Nations!

OCEAN GLOBAL FISHERIES, L.L.C.
&
SEA GLOBAL FISHERIES, L.L.C.

For the past several years, the U.S. has struggled to maintain a leadership role in the Pacific. China principally, but other nations also, have built up their influence through increased participation in commercial and political activity as well as free economic assistance. As the region has evolved and these other nations have invested heavily (both economically and diplomatically), the stark reality is that the U.S. position has not kept up with their development.

For the Pacific Island Nations, fisheries is the single most important commercial activity. The Nations seek to create sustainable fisheries for long term economic growth, which is why the U.S. fisheries remains the best opportunity to expand and enhance U.S. relationships within the region. Because of the Tuna Treaty, the U.S. tuna industry has been the Island Nations' longest commercial partner.

We are in Auckland this week attempting to revitalize the Treaty and salvage our long-standing position in the region. For the first time in many of these formal exchanges we are pleased to see a renewed vigor by the U.S. negotiating team.

There appears to be support for the Treaty among State Department officials from Washington to Papau New Guinea. However, vessel owners know that the Department of State is very complex and **we are concerned** that there are still those that don't recognize the importance of the Treaty and will not get behind this long-term agreement. Nevertheless industry members and well as delegates from American Samoa are trying to remain optimistic that we will be successful.

Mr. Chairman, this is more than a simple fisheries access arrangement. The Treaty represents the face of the United States in the Pacific region as it represents the single most important U.S. economic activity.

Our success in securing a new Treaty will send a strong signal through the region that the U.S. remains committed to the Pacific Island Nations as their allies and commercial partners. On behalf of my companies, the U.S. tuna industry and our Nation, I urge the Committee to do everything within its power to ensure that the Department of State and the other Federal agencies are successful in securing a new, updated Treaty as soon as possible.

J. Douglas Hines
Partner and Owner
Ocean Global, LLC
Sea Global, LLC